First published 2000 by Aurum Press Limited,
25 Bedford Avenue, London WC1B 3AT

A catalogue record for this book is available from the British Library.

ISBN: 1-85410-735-6

Editorial assistant: Kristina Blagojevitch
Designed by Michelle Lovric and Lisa Pentreath

Printed and bound in Italy by LEGO SpA

Poems by Stephanie June Sorréll reproduced by kind
permission of the author.

The editor gratefully acknowledges the assistance of the
following people: Judith Grant, Iain Campbell, David Franks
and Lynne Curran.

ILLUSTRATION ACKNOWLEDGEMENTS:

Front cover, detail from La Vie Seigneuriale: "La Lecture", courtesy of the musée
du Moyen-Age — Cluny, copyright © Photo RMN — G. Blot/C. Jean.
Endpapers, detail from La Dame à la Licorne: "Le Gout", courtesy of the musée
du Moyen-Age — Cluny, copyright © Photo RMN — R. G. Ojeda.
Page 19, An Orchestra of Cats Reading Music, Ferdinand van Kessel; page 30,
A Cat with her Kittens in a Basket, Samuel de Wilde, courtesy of Raphael Valls
Ltd, London.
Page 12, Le Chat, Theophile Alexandre Steinlen; page 20, A Black and White Cat,
Henriette Ronner-Knip, both courtesy of Sotheby's Picture Library, London.
Photographs by Debbie Patterson on pages 9, 10, 21 from the late Kathleen
Mann's Cat Museum, courtesy of the Executor of Kathleen Mann's estate.
Page 6, detail of the Satirical Papyrus, copyright © The British Museum.
Page 7, Egyptian cat, courtesy of The Burrell Collection, copyright © Glasgow
Museums & Art Galleries.
Page 15, Carmina Burana tapestry by Lynne Curran, reproduced courtesy of
the artist.
Victorian scraps reproduced courtesy of Mamelok Press Limited,
Bury St Edmunds, England.

Cats

To respect the cat
is the beginning
of the aesthetic sense.

Erasmus Darwin (1731—1802)
English poet and scientist

ontents

a little Book of Cats

Michelle Lovric

AURUM PRESS

Introduction

Ottoman legend has it that the Cat was created on the Ark. Noah, it seemed, gave the lion a great box on the ear, which made him sneeze, producing the cat out of his nose. In another account, the ape, bored by the monotous lifestyle of the Ark, paid his attentions to a very agreeable young lioness, whose infidelities resulted in the birth of a tom-cat and a she-cat.

Whatever its origins, the whole family of cats — the "tribe of Tiger" — shares certain traits. That universal symbol of imperial majesty, the lion, also epitomizes the peerless carnivore latent in every feline. In many places the great cats have always been held sacred. In India and Africa, villagers sometimes call the tiger who preys on them their *nene*, or grandfather, believing that the souls of their ancestors dwell inside the creature.

The cat has always been loved and feared by humans, consciously and subconsciously. Dreams of leopards are thought to be about erotic vitality, while dreams of tigers are said to reveal a longing for love but fear of sexuality. In the Japanese Shinto faith, the tiger was a holy but devouring deity. Jung saw the tiger as the symbol of female compulsion. Lions, on the other hand, are both masculine and feminine. The lion became the symbol of transformation in alchemy. In Christian terms the lion symbolizes the conversion of heretics.

In ancient Rome, the cat was a symbol of freedom. In ancient Egypt, the cat was worshipped as a symbol of the life-giving heat of the sun. Cats were mummified like esteemed humans when they died. Mohammed was said to be a lover of cats. When one settled to sleep on his robe, he cut off his sleeve rather than disturb it. The cat is presented in the legends of Buddha as the personification of wilful independence. The Japanese have always responded to the aesthetic value of the cat; for them, the beast has been a beloved icon — with one paw raised in greeting — as well as companion, for centuries. The Scandinavian goddess Frejya was said to travel the night sky in a chariot drawn by cats.

Conversely, cats have always been seen as the familiars of witches and part of Hallowe'en's dark mysteries. There have been dark times in history for cats; they were persecuted between the 13th and 18th centuries, and even burnt at the stake. But a black cat also came to symbolize good luck, especially when combined with a horseshoe.

Through the ages, poets have found cats an irresistible subject for their verse. Many writers also acknowledged cats as their muses and indispensable desk companions. Juvenile literature overflows with cat personalities, each demonstrating an aspect of the feline temperament: the cunning Puss in Boots, the mischievous Three Little Kittens and, of course, the enigmatic Cheshire Cat in Lewis Carroll's *Alice's Adventures in Wonderland.* Rudyard Kipling described the uncompromising independence at the core of every feline in *The Cat that Walked by Himself.* Edward Lear firmly established the cat as a creature of luxury and romance in "The Owl and the Pussy Cat".

It is not known when the cat was adopted as a family pet. At first cats were welcomed into human habitations to exterminate the vermin, but the relationship eventually became more emotional. In the course of the 19th century, both Britain and America became nations of cat-keepers, taking their lead from Queen Victoria, who owned a pair of Persians. The very first cat shows took place at Crystal Palace in London in 1871 and in Madison Square Garden in New York in 1895.

Louis Wain, the most famous Victorian cat artist, used cats to depict all the human virtues and the Seven Deadly Sins. Cats were seen to embody human values more than any other animal. The cat was thought to be a great and persistent lover. The strong maternal instinct of the cat has ever been praised. The comedy played out by kittens has always been enjoyed as a spectacle of innocent joy.

While cats have been worshipped since ancient times, it is only relatively recently that they have come to be loved and cherished as domestic pets. In this paradox of distance and intimacy, we see the ambivalence of our relationship with cats — and their relationship with us. We find cats unfathomable, indolent, over-sexed and indifferent, but we also find them irresistible in their elegance, beauty, affection and mystery.

Cat Lore

It is not a little singular that the origin of the most important member of this family, the domestic cat *(Felis domestica)* should be involved in such obscurity. By the older naturalists it was supposed that it might be considered to be descended from the wild cat *(Felis catus-ferus)*. Modern science has upset this theory by bringing a tremendous array of argument, and battering at its most vulnerable parts. In its place another theory has been substituted, and accepted generally ... It is well known that the ancient Egyptians possessed a domestic animal, which, judging from re-presentations of it on the monuments of Thebes and elsewhere, bore a resemblance to our domestic cat ... This same animal has been referred to as being not unlikely the progenitor of the domestic cat.

from *Beeton's Dictionary of Natural History*, 1871.

From the dawn of creation the cat has known his place, and he has kept it, practically untamed and unspoiled by man.

Andrew Lang (1844—1912)
Scottish man of letters

Among the curious features connected with the association of the cat with man, we may note that it is the only animal which has been tolerated, esteemed, and at times worshipped, without having a single distinctly valuable quality.

Nathaniel Southgate Shaler (1841—1906)
American writer

All cats were at first wild, but were at length tamed ... it is a Beast of prey, even the tame one, more especially the wild, it being in the opinion of many nothing but a diminutive lyon.

William S. Salmon (1644—1713)
English writer

CAT REMEDIES

Against eye diseases: ashes from the burnt head of a black cat.
Against shingles: cat's blood mixed with milk.
Against consumption: stewed black-cat gravy.
Against whooping cough: swallowing hairs from a black cat's tail.
Against toothache: holding a dried cat skin over the face.

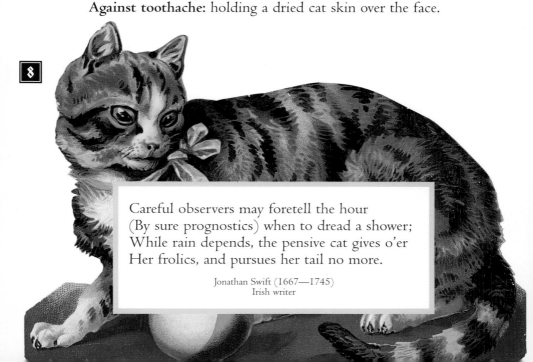

Careful observers may foretell the hour
(By sure prognostics) when to dread a shower;
While rain depends, the pensive cat gives o'er
Her frolics, and pursues her tail no more.

Jonathan Swift (1667—1745)
Irish writer

CAT SUPERSTITIONS

BAD LUCK

A cat jumping on the table; meeting a black cat at dawn; a black cat turning its back on you; hearing a cat's voice before setting off on a journey.

Drowning a cat: the devil will take revenge.

Seeing two cats fighting: for a sick person, this means death.

A cat jumping over a corpse: the corpse will become a vampire.

Kicking a cat: rheumatism will ensue.

GOOD LUCK

Being given a black cat, meeting three black cats in succession; touching a black cat; having the family cat at your wedding; having a cat at the theatre; a cat sneezing once.

A cat washing its right ear: a male stranger will come.

A cat washing its left ear: a female stranger will come.

A three-coloured cat: protects a house from fire.

CAT DREAMS

Dreaming of cats: lust and self-will for women, particularly.

A sick person dreaming of cats: death.

Cats' tongues

Proverbs & Sayings

In cat's eyes, all things belong to cats.

English proverb

Trouble is like a cat's back. There's two ways to stroke it.

Yorkshire proverb

I can do that too, said the tom cat when he saw the camel, and he made a hump on his back.

German proverb

The cat doesn't meow when the dog is bitten by fleas.

German proverb

All cats are bad in May.

French proverb

The noses of cats, the knees of men, and the bottoms of women are always cold.

Venetian proverb

THE CAT KNOWS WHOSE LIPS SHE LICKS.

Latin proverb

Every dog has his day and a cat two Sundays.

English proverb

I gave an order to a cat, and the cat gave it to its tail.

Chinese proverb

CAT SLANG

Cat call: a kind of whistle, chiefly used at theatres, to interrupt the actors, and damn a new piece ... greatly resembles the modulations of an intriguing boar cat.

Cat in pan: to turn cat in pan: to change sides or parties.

Cat's foot: to live under the cat's foot: to be under the dominion of a wife, hen-pecked.

As many lives as a cat: cats, according to vulgar naturalists, have nine lives, that is, one less than a woman.

Cat lap: tea, also called scandal broth.

Cat's paw: to be made a cat's paw of: to be made a tool or instrument to accomplish the purpose of another; an allusion to the story of a monkey, who made use of a cat's paw to scratch a roasted chestnut out of the fire.

Cat's sleep: counterfeit sleep: cats often counterfeit sleep to decoy their prey near them, and suddenly spring on them.

Cat sticks: thin legs, compared to sticks with which boys play at cat.

Francis Grose (1731—91)
English antiquary
from *A Classical Dictionary of the Vulgar Tongue*, 1785.

Cat, Cat
What are you?

Amy Lowell (1874—1925)
American poet

The nature of cats

Of all animals, he alone attains the Contemplative Life.

Andrew Lang (1844—1912)
Scottish man of letters

I've met many thinkers and many cats,
but the wisdom of cats is infinitely superior.

Hippolyte Taine (1828—93)
French historian and critic

It is not even necessary to mention his name, for he seems to know instinctively whether he is the object of conversation; and if he is spoken of in a manner grateful to his feelings, he openly plumes himself on the good opinion that he hears, or sometimes pretends to be asleep, though the slight winking of one eye proves very plainly that he is awake.

Reverend John George Wood (1827—89)
English naturalist and writer

Who can believe that there is no soul behind those luminous eyes!

Théophile Gautier (1811—72)
French writer

A cat may look at a king;— yes; but can it *see* a king when it looks at him? ... when a cat caresses you, it never looks at you. Its heart seems to be in its back and paws, not its eyes. It will rub itself against you, or pat you with velvet tufts, instead of talons, but you may talk to it for an hour altogether, yet not rightly catch its eye.

John Ruskin (1819—1900)
English writer, artist, designer and philosopher

It is easy to understand why the rabble dislike cats.
A cat is beautiful; it suggests ideas of luxury, cleanliness,
voluptuous pleasures.

Charles Pierre Baudelaire (1821—67)
French poet

She is like the lady of fashion who so directs her affairs that all necessary work shall be performed by someone else and her own time left free for pleasure.

Georgina Stickland Gates
from *The Modern Cat: Her Mind and Manners*, 1928.

Floret siva in bis Flores et foliis

vbi est antiqvvs meus amor

15

They are very like women in their reactions — clever women ...
They are uncontrollable — they only do what they please. They
are timid and brave — selfish and indifferent, self-seeking,
cupboard-loving — graceful, mysterious, vindictive — passionate
and voluptuous. Sensuous always, sensual at moments. Contrary
— and infinitely fascinating ...

Elinor Glyn (1864—1943)
English novelist

Catalogue
Shapes & Styles of Cats

I firmly believe that the cat is very proud of her appearance, and likes to cut a dash.

William Gordon Stables (1840—1910)
Scottish writer

You never could convince a Cat that she was *not* pretty or graceful or attractive ...

Alfred Elwes
from *The Adventures of a Cat, And a Fine Cat, Too!*, 1857.

He seems the incarnation of everything soft and silky and velvety, without a sharp edge in his composition ...

Saki (Hector Hugo Munro) (1870—1916)
British writer

SOME OF THE SPECIES ON DISPLAY AT THE GREAT CRYSTAL PALACE CAT SHOW

Tortoiseshell Cats are, as a rule, neither very large, nor very prepossessing. They have a sinister look about them, as though they would as soon bite you as not.

Brown Tabby. This is a class of very fine, noble cats. They are true English cats, and, if well trained, possess all pussy's noblest attributes to perfection. They are docile, honest, and faithful, fond of children, careful mothers and brave fathers ... and it is of them nearly all the best cat stories are told.

Spotted Tabby. A large "sonsy" animal, with broad brow and chest, short ears, and well-pleased face, quite the cat to sing lullabies at the farmer's fireside, or to romp in the garden or on the parlour floor with the squire's bright-eyed English children.

Black and White. A large, handsome gentlemanlike fellow, a sort of cat that you could not believe would condescend to do a dirty action, or would hardly deign to capture a miserable mouse; and his wife is a perfect lady.

Black. Colour to be entirely black; no white. No, not a morsel of white can be here tolerated, not even on the point of the chin; although we often see pure black cats on whose coats Nature seems to have been amusing herself, by planting long single white hairs all over them.

William Gordon Stables (1840—1910)
Scottish writer

For there is nothing brisker than his life when in motion.

Christopher Smart (1722—71)
English poet

One minute quicksilver, next minute butterballs,
Precise as a fencer, lax as an odalisque ...

Louis MacNeice (1907—63)
Irish poet

Slowly,
slowly,
You rise
and stretch
In a glossiness
of beautiful
curves ...

Amy Lowell (1874—1925)
American poet

In the word part of the language of the Cat there are, probably, not more than six hundred fundamental words, all others being derivatives. Consonants are daintily used, while a wide berth is given to explosives and the liquid letters "l" and "r" enter into the great majority of sounds.

Marvin R. Clark
from *Pussy and Her Language*, 1896.

How dear is the hearthstone, so laughing and warm!
Where my cat sits composing her puritan face ...

John Critchley Prince (1808—66)
English poet

 Cat Love

Cats must be trained when young;
and the very first thing you must teach them is *to love you.*

William Gordon Stables (1840—1910)
Scottish writer

Once it has given its love, what absolute confidence, what fidelity of affection! It will make of itself the companion of your hours of work, of loneliness, or of sadness. It will lie the whole evening on your knee ... leaving the company of creatures of its own society to be with you.

Théophile Gautier (1811—72)
French writer

What is the source of the love she bears me? ... She has the modesty that belongs to perfect lovers, and their dread of too insistent contacts. I shall not say much more about her. All the rest is silence, faithfulness, impacts of soul, the shadow of an azure shape on the blue paper that receives everything I write, the silent passage of paws silvered with moisture.

Sidonie Gabrielle Colette (1873—1954)
French novelist

THE SILENT PURR

Oh — big human friend,
you think I am so far removed
from your fears and doubts
that I cannot understand
your disappointments.
But, if you will look into my eyes
as I am beseeching you to do now,
you will see the nakedness of my soul,
and find your own vulnerability reflected.
So please, in your lofty aspirations,
don't overlook the invisible gifts
I bring you.
Today I watched the wind
whirling the snowflakes
about in a chaotic dance of white radiance.
The flakes reminded me of your feathered dreams,
and my excited paws rushed up to your desk to
share the magical soundless dance with you;
hoping that through my throaty message you
too could experience the joy I have found ...
just gaze into my eyes, be still —
and I will purr deep within your soul ...

Stephanie June Sorréll (b. 1956)
English poet

To gain the friendship of a cat is not an easy thing ...
It does not give its affections indiscriminately.
It will consent to be your friend if you are worthy
of the honour, but it will not be your slave.

Théophile Gautier (1811—72)
French writer

Philosopher and comrade, not for thee
The fond and foolish love which binds the dog;
Only a quiet sympathy which sees
Through all my faults, and bears with them awhile.
Be lenient still, and have some faith in me,
Gentlest of sceptics, sleepiest of friends.

François Élie Jules Lemaître (1853—1914)
French playwright and critic

Cats' paws
Appetites & Instincts

She sights a Bird — she chuckles —
She flattens — then she crawls —
She runs without the look of feet —
Her eyes increase to Balls —

Her Jaws stir — twitching — hungry —
Her Teeth can hardly stand —
She leaps, but Robin leaped the first —
Ah, Pussy, of the Sand,

The Hopes so juicy ripening —
You almost bathed your Tongue —
When Bliss disclosed a hundred Wings —
And fled with every one —

Emily Dickinson (1830—86)
American poet

The cat was lying on the ground. Suddenly, she turned into a dragon, into a flame, into a flying fish, and under her belly, between her silver paws, I saw a green lizard appear as though she had just that moment invented it.

Sidonie Gabrielle Colette (1873—1954)
French novelist

Smite the Sudden Spool, and spring
Upon the Swift Elusive String,
Thus you learn to catch the wary
Mister Mouse or Miss Canary.

Oliver Herford (1863—1935)
American humorist and writer

25

Badly-housed cats become vagrants and thieves ... plunder pigeon lofts, steal chickens, tear up beautiful flower-beds, and murder valuable rabbits in cold blood ... A cat that has been well fed and cared for by day, will seldom want to go out at night. If she does not feel sleepy, she will betake herself to the cellar, and have a little innocent flirtation with the mice or rats, or kill cockroaches when everything else fails her.

William Gordon Stables (1840—1910)
Scottish writer

I regret to say that Pret has one fault ... if he can steal anything eatable, he will do so. Not because he is hungry, but merely for his own amusement, does he scent out, steal, and hide something that has been carefully concealed from him; just as youthful aristocrats were, in former days, accustomed to steal door-knockers and bell handles, not for any pecuniary value which they might possess, but simply as tangible proof of their nocturnal prowess.

Reverend John George Wood (1827—89)
English naturalist and writer

EVERY PUSSY, IF GIVEN

27

CHANCE, IS AN EPICURE.

Beverley Nichols (1898—1983) English writer

Caterwauls

the Love Life of Cats

When the cat's away, it's probably mating.

Eva Gabor (1921—95)
Hungarian-born American actress

He is a full lecherous beast in youth, swift, pliant and merry ...

Bartholomeus Anglicus
from *De Proprietatibus Rerum*, c. 1260.

Cats, of course, are determined fighters, but these fights are like the romantic combats of chivalry, or the brabbles of the *apaches* of modern Paris: they are broils over the female of the species. For the cat is a great lover.

Carl Van Vechten (1880—1964)
American writer and photographer

The female commonly gallantizes the Male.

Denis de Coetlogon
from *A Tour Through the Animal World*, 1746.

From among the great variety of *myows* (sixty-three can be counted, but the notation of them is difficult) I will select one that is particularly expressive, and accompanied by so precise a gesture that it can only be translated into "are you coming?" Then with one accord the cats adjourn to an adjoining room, or to the housetop, and interchange the most ardent vows.

Champfleury (Jules Fleury-Husson) (1821—89)
French writer

Cats' Cradles
the maternal cat

It is the cry that a cat makes only for her kittens —
a soft trilling coo — a pure caress of tone.

Lafcadio Hearn (1856—1904)
Greek/Irish writer

When they bring into the world two or three blind, squeaking kittens with little quivering tails, there begins the eternal spectacle of maternal love. Your cat overflowing with gentleness and dignity, lying on her side, curled round so that her whole body and all four paws are protecting her shivering offspring, and making herself their cave, home and furry bed.

Karel Čapek (1890—1938)
Czech journalist and writer

On April 5th our one daffodil came into flower & our cat, Charlie Chaplin, had a kitten ... I attended the birth. Charles implored me. He behaved so strangely; he became a beautiful tragic figure with blue-green eyes, terrified and wild. He would only lie still when I stroked his belly & said: "it's all right, old chap. It's bound to happen to a man sooner or later." And, in the middle of his pangs, his betrayer, a wretch of a cat with a face like a penny bun & the cat-equivalent of a brown bowler hat, rather rakish over one ear, began to *howl* from outside. Fool that I have been! said Charles, grinding his claws against my sleeve. The second kitten April was born during the night, a sunny compact little girl. When she sucks she looks like a small infant saying its prayers & *knowing* that Jesus loves her. She always has her choice of the strawberry, the chocolate and the pistachio one; poor little Athenaeum has to put up with an occasional grab at the lemon one ... They are both loves; their paws inside are very soft, very pink, just like unripe raspberries.

Katherine Mansfield (1888—1923)
New Zealand-born writer

Kittenhood

I have a kitten, my dear, the drollest of all creatures that ever wore a cat's skin.

William Cowper (1731—1800)
English poet

Kittenhood, the baby time, especially of country cats, is with most the brightest, sprightliest, and prettiest period of their existence, and perhaps the most happy.

Harrison Weir (1824—1906)
English animal artist and writer

"Life!" said the Kitten, winking her eyes,
And twitching her tail, in a droll surprise —
"Life? — Oh, it's racing over the floor,
Out at the window and in at the door;
Now on the chair-back, now on the table,
'Mid balls of cotton and skeins of silk,
And crumbs of sugar and jugs of milk ...

Thomas Westwood (1814—58)
English poet

Here is a Persian kitten behaving herself very badly. She has got into the larder and seated herself on a large pie, and what terrible mischief she is causing. There are four glasses of jelly and cream, and a glass butter-dish as well as a biscuit-tin. She has upset one glass, and now she is seated on the pie-crust and having such a feast of whipped cream that she never had in her life before.

Mrs H. B. Paull
from *The Greedy Kitten*, 1890.

Witches' cats

"I've heard my mother say that there ain't a cat mentioned in the whole Bible, from beginning to end. You just lay that to heart, and have nothing to do with cats."

W. L. Alden
from *Cat Tales*, 1905.

Black Cats and skulls have always been associated with magic and witchcraft, the most powerful weapon for spells being the skull of a black Cat that had been fed on human flesh.

Charles Platt
from *"Mieaou!" A Treatise on Cats*, 1934.

The familiars of witches do most ordinarily appear in the shape of cats, which is an argument that the beast is dangerous to soul and body.

Edward Topsell (?—1638)
English religious writer

Cats are a mysterious kind of folk. There is more passing in their minds than we are aware of. It comes no doubt from their being so familiar with warlocks and witches.

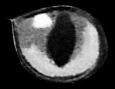

Sir Walter Scott
(1771—1832)
Scottish novelist
and poet

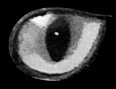

It was believed that the devil borrowed the black coat of the cat when he wanted to torment his victims ... the large, fixed, green eyes of the animal had something to do with its terribly bad reputation.

Champfleury (Jules Fleury-Husson) (1821—89) French writer

In some of the more unfrequented districts of Scotland, the good folks are still very careful to shut up their cats in the house, on Hallowe'en, *i.e.,* the 31st of October. And they tell me, that those cats that have managed to escape incarceration, that night may be seen, by those brave enough to look, scampering over hill and dell, and across the lonely moors, each one ridden by a brownie, a bogle, a spunkie, or some other infernal jockey, in fact, a devil's own steeplechase.

William Gordon Stables (1840—1910)
Scottish writer

Great cats

I have the jungle in my heart.

Gellett Burgess
(1866—1951)
American humorist
and illustrator

The lion is called the king of the beasts. His figure is striking; his look bold and confident, and his voice terrible. He has a very broad face, surrounded with a long mane, which gives him a peculiarly majestic aspect; his eyes are bright and fiery, and his tongue is beset with prickles as hard as a cat's claw.

from *Natural History*, 1823.

In many places the inhabitants appear to have resigned the dominion to the tigers, and take few precautions against them, regarding them as sacred. The natives hold the transmigration of souls, and call the tiger their *nene*, or grandfather, upon the supposition that the souls of their ancestors are dwelling in the tigers.

from *Beeton's Dictionary of Natural History*, 1871.

I no longer want to marry anyone, but I still dream that I am marrying a very big cat.

Sidonie Gabrielle Cole
(1873—1954)
French novelist

In The Faerie Queen, *Una, the princess, chances on a lion, while travelling alone in wild country ...*

It fortuned, out of the thickest wood
A ramping Lyon rushed suddeinly,
Hunting full greedy after salvage blood.
Soone as the royall virgin he did spy,
With gaping mouth at her ran greedily,
To have attonce devoured her tender corse;
But to the pray when as he drew more ny,
His bloody rage aswaged with remorse,
And, with the sight amazd, forgat his furious forse.

In stead thereof he kist her wearie feet,
And lickt her lilly hands with fawning tong,
As he her wronged innocence did weet.
O, how can beautie maister the most strong,
And simple truth subdue avenging wrong! ...

The Lyon would not leave her desolate,
But with her went along, as a strong gard
Of her chast person, and a faythfull mate
Of her sad troubles and misfortunes hard:
Still, when she slept, he kept both watch and ward;
And, when she wakt, he wayted diligent,
With humble service to her will prepard:
From her fayre eyes he tooke commandement,
And ever by her lookes conceived her intent ...

Edmund Spenser (c. 1552—99)
English poet

Making the cat laugh

To speak of the cat as a humorist, in any shape of form, sounds, I admit, something very like a contradiction in terms ... Even granted that the cat has herself little or no primary sense of humour, she is capable, when properly understood, of affording intense amusement to others. To realize this fact is a great source of pleasure — nay, of security. It is, indeed, hardly too much to say that unless some means are discovered for taking her down a peg or two every now and then, a cat is an impossible beast to live with. Her pomposity, her formality, and her *de haut en bas* manner of looking at the world, would be unbearable unless we knew how on occasion to turn the laugh against her.

from *Cat and Bird Stories* from "The Spectator", 1896.

Cats only play the fool at certain times and I do not know
the rules they play by.

Alice Thomas Ellis
Contemporary English writer

FOR HE IS A MIXTURE
OF GRAVITY AND WAGGERY

Christopher Smart
(1722—71)
English poet

But does this explain why the yellow kitten, as it
followed me about the garden, spent some minutes in
quarrelling with a pansy? The pansy lifted an inane,
purple face towards the sky, and its head waggled
helplessly on its stalk. The yellow kitten sat down beside
it, and regarded it severely for awhile. Then he slapped
its silly face.

Margaret Benson
from *The Soul of a Cat and Other Stories*, 1901.

Requiescat

TIGER'S LAST CALL

I am already leaving.
With these words I will have left a little more.
Only your heart can halt the hourglass and invite me to stay.
With these paws I have loved the earth;
imprinting it with my hunger, my strength, my beauty.
To this earth, I have added my children,
my life, my blood, my death.
My whiskers have dowsed the knowledge of my ancestors.
My roar contains their fire.
Once I am gone, so are my ancestors, and my future.
If you cut off your past, then you too forfeit your future
so that your soul bleeds empty in the present.
I bear no blame nor shame.
I stand strong in my memories
and walk beside you in your dreams.

I am almost gone now
The hourglass overflows.
Only your heart can invite me to stay.

Stephanie June Sorréll (b. 1956)
English poet

A CATALECTIC MONODY!

A cat I sing, of famous memory,
Though *cat*achrestical my song may be;
In a small garden *cat*acomb she lies,
And *cat*aclysms fill her comrades' eyes;
Borne on the air, the *cat*acoustic song
Swells with her virtues' *cat*alogue along,
No *cat*aplasm could lengthen out her years,
Though mourning friends shed *cat*aracts of tears.

George Cruikshank (1792—1878)
English artist and engraver